IMAGES
of America

MOUNT RAINIER'S HISTORIC INNS AND LODGES

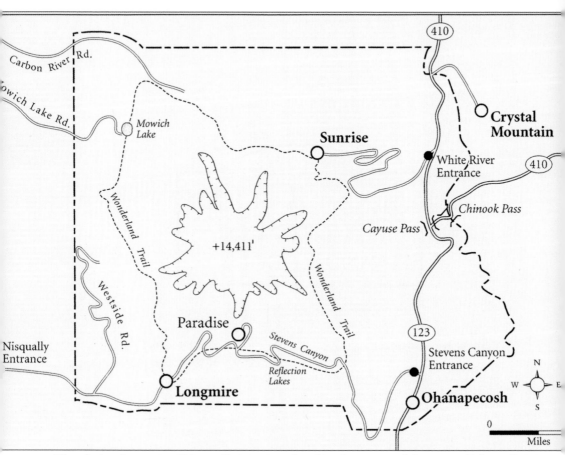

The glaciated summit of Mount Rainier is outlined in the center of this map of Mount Rainier National Park. Points of interest shown here, such as Longmire, Paradise, Ohanapecosh, and Sunrise, are featured in this story of change and preservation at one of the United States' most beautiful places. (Courtesy of and used with permission from the University of Washington Press.)

ON THE COVER: For 100 years, Paradise Inn has welcomed generation after generation to its subalpine meadow location in Mount Rainier National Park. The steeply pitched roof, dormer windows, and timbered porch complement the surrounding natural environment beautifully. Those lucky enough to spend time in this special place do not soon forget it! (Courtesy of Mount Rainier National Park Archives.)

IMAGES
of America

MOUNT RAINIER'S HISTORIC INNS AND LODGES

Jeff and Sonja Anderson

ARCADIA
PUBLISHING

Copyright © 2017 by Jeff and Sonja Anderson
ISBN 978-1-4671-2487-4

Published by Arcadia Publishing
Charleston, South Carolina

Printed in the United States of America

Library of Congress Control Number: 2017932978

For all general information, please contact Arcadia Publishing:
Telephone 843-853-2070
Fax 843-853-0044
E-mail sales@arcadiapublishing.com
For customer service and orders:
Toll-Free 1-888-313-2665

Visit us on the Internet at www.arcadiapublishing.com

In gratitude to the visionaries who worked to restore and preserve Mount Rainier National Park as a wilderness playground in all of its natural splendor.

CONTENTS

ACKNOWLEDGMENTS

This book would not have been possible without the generous and capable help of the Mount Rainier National Park Archives staff archivist Brooke Childrey. We would also like to thank National Park Service museum intern Kelly Teal and volunteer Ann Spillane for their hours of help selecting and scanning the images. Our days spent at the archives were a real delight. Unless otherwise noted, all images appearing in this book were graciously provided by the Mount Rainier National Park Archives. Also, we'd like to thank National Park Service rangers Amber Sergent and Logan Wegmeyer and outreach specialist Jim Ross for engaging our questions. We are grateful to Connie Hellyer and her family for sharing their images of the Paradise Ski Tow. Cheryl Gunselman at Washington State University and Puja Boyd at the University of Washington Press were both helpful as we tried to track down different maps of the park. Thanks also go to our daughter, Amanda, who spent precious vacation time cheerfully going through box after box of black-and-white images and proofreading the manuscript.

We are especially grateful to the people who first introduced us to "the mountain." For Jeff, it was his parents, especially his late father, Stanley Anderson, who fondly remembered skiing at Paradise as a young adult. He loved to tell about a watermelon left in the snow, only to later discover it sitting on top of a snow pedestal when he returned! We all learned about mountain snowmelt from that story. For Sonja, her North Park College friend Linda Hedin Larson took her hiking at Sunrise, proudly showing her the place she had talked about over dinner in their Midwest college cafeteria. We cherish all our memories at Mount Rainier and are grateful for out-of-town guests who give us an excuse to return to the mountain again and again.

INTRODUCTION

The mountain has always been there. Growing up in Burien, a community south of Seattle, "the Mountain"—as locals often refer to Mount Rainier—was ever present. Walking to school, going to the store, trips to Seattle, Des Moines, Kent, Renton—all included views of the mountain. Crossing Puget Sound on a ferry, traveling across Lake Washington on the floating bridges, heading to the airport—mountain, mountain, mountain. Sure, views were often shrouded by clouds in the famously gray Northwest climate, but somehow, that made the mountain still more magical, like a sentry watching in the night.

Mount Rainier commands attention, standing at 14,411 feet. This is 13,210 feet above its surrounding area (and pretty much more than 14,000 feet considering the surrounding metropolitan areas are at sea level). Native American tribes held a mystical view of the mountain. Like other mountains, it was thought to possess a hostile power not to be toyed with. However, early settlers (like tourists today) were drawn to the mountain, and in 1870, Philemon Beecher Van Trump and Hazard Stevens completed the first recorded ascent.

Thirteen years later, a settler from Indiana living in Yelm Prairie, James Longmire, returned from an ascent and stumbled across hot springs while looking for his horse. That area bears the Longmire family name to this day. He and his family established a hospitality business focused on the supposed curative properties of the natural springs. The legacy of the Longmire enterprise was the creation of roads and trails, opening new opportunities for visitors, including access to Paradise—what would become the crown jewel of the future national park.

Travel to the mountain was difficult in the early years. One could travel from Seattle to Tacoma via steamship or train and then board a train to Ashford. From Ashford, visitors traveled by horseback and, after 1884, by wagon to the Longmire Medical Springs resort on a rough road built by the Longmires. This was a vast improvement from the two-day hike from Tacoma to the springs. Later, the Longmires completed a rough road from their hotel to Paradise, a distance of about 11 miles. One of the first cars to travel an improved road to Paradise carried Pres. William Howard Taft. It did not complete the distance without the help of mules to pull the car.

With roads, lodging and other amenities naturally followed. However, there needed to be an organizing entity to make that happen. Congress created Mount Rainier National Park in 1899, but the National Park Service did not come into existence until 1916. Development during this period was haphazard. While significant, the Longmire operation was not well funded and of rather poor quality. Tacoma Eastern Railroad provided new leadership by building the high-quality National Park Inn near the Longmires' enterprise. Then, in 1917, the New Longmire Springs Hotel, built by new investors, opened right across the street from the National Park Inn.

At the same time, the Rainier National Park Company (RNPC) was organized by business interests in Tacoma and Seattle with the support of Stephen Mather, director of the National Park Service. This group provided development leadership throughout the park until 1940, when it sold its properties to the federal government; however, RNPC retained leasing rights until 1968, when it dissolved. The work of the RNPC was impressive. Consolidating the various enterprises, the group at Longmire purchased the National Park Inn, moved the new Longmire Springs Hotel in 1920 across the street next to the National Park Inn, renamed it the National Park Inn Annex, and took over the old Longmire Springs Hotel. That hotel burned down in 1920. When the National Park Inn burned to the ground in 1926, the annex was renamed the National Park Inn, as we know it today.

At Paradise, the RNPC opened Paradise Inn on July 1, 1917, and it remains the grand lodge of the park. In 1920, the RNPC added a guest room annex behind the inn. Paradise Camp Lodge (in the same approximate location as today's Henry M. Jackson Memorial Visitor Center) opened in 1918 and was enlarged in 1925. Later called the Tatoosh club, Paradise Camp Lodge was demolished for parking in the mid-1950s. Two buildings, Paradise Lodge and Ski Dorm, were built primarily for winter activities since the location of Paradise Inn was susceptible to snowdrifting and could not be kept open during the winter. Paradise Lodge opened in 1928, then was intentionally burned in 1965 for parking at the new Paradise Visitor Center. Ski Dorm opened in 1941 to provide a more affordable venue for groups. It was converted to house concessionaire and park service employees in 1964.

The Paradise Visitor Center, later renamed Henry M. Jackson Visitor Center, was opened in 1966. It was a beautiful building nestled in the hillside, echoing the shape of the mountain with amazing views of the Tatoosh Range as well as Mount Rainier. However, a poorly designed roof required 300 to 500 gallons of diesel fuel per day during the winter season to prevent it from collapsing due to heavy snow. The present Henry M. Jackson Memorial Visitor Center opened in 2008.

Elsewhere in the park, N.D. Tower started Ohanapecosh Hot Springs in 1921. He was later joined by Dr. Albert W. Bridge, a physician who practiced in Eatonville and Tacoma and whose estate provided key funding for Mary Bridge Children's Hospital in Tacoma. By 1935, a road from Packwood, a small lodge, bathhouse, and eventually, a cluster of cabins were built. The park boundary included the area in 1931. Falling into disrepair, the resort closed in 1960, and buildings were removed by 1967.

Sunrise Day Lodge opened in 1931. It was originally planned by the Rainier National Park Company to be grander than Paradise Inn with the help of railroad investors. The $2 million venture was later rejected by the railroad investors due to the Great Depression. The South Blockhouse was completed in 1931, with the North Blockhouse and visitor center completed in 1943.

The mountain is a gift from God to us all to respect, protect, and enjoy. It is remarkably accessible for a peak of its size and grandeur; the 104-mile trip from Seattle to Paradise can be driven in less than three hours. Both rugged and graceful, it inspires great ambition and awe. Naturalist John Muir said of the mountain:

> Of all the fire mountains which like beacons, once blazed along the Pacific Coast, Mount Rainier is the noblest. . . . Every one of these parks, great and small, is a garden filled knee-deep with fresh, lovely flowers of every hue, the most luxuriant and the most extravagantly beautiful of all the alpine gardens I ever beheld in all my mountain-top wanderings.

We are indebted to those who labored to give us access to the mountain; we understand those who wanted to use it as an entertainment centerpiece, but we are grateful to the visionaries who understood the frailty of this powerful place and worked to preserve it for us and later generations to share and enjoy its natural state.

The mountain calls. Come to the mountain.

One

TAKING THE "WATER CURE"

Welcome to Mount Rainier National Park! Imagine a time when there were no roads to drive on, no entrance gate to drive under, and indeed, no way to get to the mountain except through long, difficult hikes or bumpy rides on packhorses. A journey to visit Mount Rainier in the mid-1800s was nothing short of an expedition.

Today's visitors owe much to this man, James Longmire, an early settler to the new Washington Territory. Co-captain of the first wagon train over old Naches Pass in 1853, Longmire moved his wife and four children from Shawnee Prairie, Indiana, to a new life in sparsely settled Yelm Prairie. The journey was difficult and included the following trials: 30 hungry wolves competing with him for newly killed buffalo meat (the wolves won), nearly drowning while crossing a river with his cattle, and helping lower wagon after wagon down a steep, 300-foot embankment with rope. Longmire fully appreciated the beautiful country where he found himself at the journey's end. He called the "majestic mountain . . . standing guard over all in its snowy coat" a "scene for the artist's brush, the most beautiful I had ever seen, and good enough for me."

10

One of James Longmire's sons, Elcaine (seated on the first horse, with the staff and long beard), leads a pack train of visitors into the area now known as Mount Rainier National Park. James and his family explored much of the area looking for mineral deposits. In 1861, they built a rough trail from Yelm to Bear Prairie (so named for the bear he killed there).

Fellow Yelm Prairie settler Philemon Beecher Van Trump made the first recorded ascent of Mount Rainier in 1870. Describing the area as a "howling wilderness," Van Trump called on Longmire to guide him and others on a second attempt in 1883. Longmire's wife pleaded, "Jim, you jest shan't go!" However, it was on this trip that he discovered the bubbling mineral springs that changed all their lives.

Members of this early climbing party are recorded as, from left to right, Amsden, Leonard Longmire, Fay Fuller, and E.C. Smith. "Len" Longmire, as he was typically called, acted as guide for many climbs, reportedly collecting $1 from each climber.

Fay Fuller, a teacher from Yelm, created quite a stir summiting Rainier with several men. Later, she wrote mountaineering articles for her father's Tacoma newspaper, eventually helping form the Mazamas, who advocated for establishing Mount Rainier as a national park. Visitors today owe much to early climbers for their writings, speeches, and lantern slide presentations that helped create enthusiasm for a national park.

After discovering several different bubbling springs in the meadow where his horses strayed during the 1883 climb, James Longmire rushed home and announced, "Well, boys, I've found my fortune." He sent some bottles of water from the springs to Chicago to be analyzed for mineral content. When he received the results, he filed a mineral claim and was awarded 18.2 acres of land. Pictured here is a sulphur spring.

This spring is called Soda Springs. To reach it, Longmire had to cut a 60-mile line through "virgin timber" by hand, using just an ax, a saw, and a maul. He worked hard for his family's future prosperity. One grandchild fondly remembered that he not only worked diligently, but he "looked a lot like Abraham Lincoln, just as homely but as good and as highly respected."

Red pigments stain the spring pictured here, called Iron Mike. Cold, pure water high above Longmire filters through the earth, is warmed by the geothermal heat within the mountain, and makes its way back toward the surface. When the hot water swirls past rocks with iron content, it dissolves into the water where it ultimately oxidizes (rusts) upon air contact.

Believing, like others at the time, in the health-giving qualities of mineral spring waters, James Longmire soon erected a rustic, two-story hotel of split cedar. Five small bedrooms on the second floor hosted guests for 50¢ a bed. Meals were 25¢. Outbuildings to house more guests as well as horses and supplies, such as fresh meat, were built as necessary.

In this image of Longmire Springs Bathhouse, two women stand in front of signs that read, "Bath House" and "Mineral Baths." Where the hot springs bubbled up, the Longmires dug a hole about three feet by six feet. Then, they sunk a wooden frame down into the hole. Slats on the bottom let the water bubble up, and a ditch carried off the excess flow. The family advertised Longmire's Medical Springs to the local community, calling it "an antidote for Disease, prepared in Nature's Own Laboratory." An advertisement in *Every Sunday* on August 9, 1890, said that people could reach the springs by first taking the Northern Pacific Railroad to Yelm and then by riding "gentle saddle-horses." Trains of saddle horses departed on the first and fifteenth of August and September, and the cost for a round trip was $12. Board and treatment at the springs cost $8 per week.

Virinda Longmire, James's wife, stands with a staff in one hand and a cup of spring water in the other. Guests recalled her hearty, family-style meals. For her stove, James took flat rocks from the bottom of the river, put them together with mortar, and covered them with a piece of sheet iron. Her fresh-baked bread was legendary, and one grandchild recalled her huckleberry dumplings with cream. For breakfast, a guest could expect ham and eggs, fried potatoes, and hot cakes. Dinner was often wild game. The couple shown below is Elcaine Longmire, James's son, and his wife, Martha, who were very involved in the family business.

Elcaine and his son Leonard built this log cabin in 1888; it is the oldest structure still standing in the park today. Restored in the 1930s by the Civilian Conservation Corps (CCC), it was originally used during the summer to keep watch over the nearby meat house. To refrigerate the inn's meat, river water was piped in, keeping the meat cold through evaporation. Later, ice was brought to the inn from Nisqually Glacier.

This ice cream concession stand was tucked among erratics (glacier-dropped boulders) near Nisqually Glacier. A sign reads, "Royal Ice Cream." The entrepreneurial Longmire family operated this and several other businesses, including a pack train service for guests from the Yelm and Ashford rail stops, a grocery store and confectionery, and even a tavern, which the National Park Service immediately shut down as a "public nuisance."

The sign above the tables reads, "Camp Thomas & Tappan." Activities in the early days in the Longmire area were simple, with picnics being popular. Note the man slicing the watermelon, which has been a picnic staple for generations. Picnicking is still popular with day visitors at many locations around the mountain.

Comparing this image of the Longmire Springs Hotel to the one on page 14 shows many changes. A second story was added to the original section on the far left, and a second story and porch were added on the far right. Despite the challenges getting to the springs and its primitive resort conditions, this was a popular destination for adventuresome tourists from the growing cities of Tacoma and Seattle.

In 1890, the Longmires built a trail from Longmire Springs to Paradise. This image shows the tent cabin "hotel" that accommodated not only tourists who came for the mineral baths but also those on their way up the mountain. In 1915, campgrounds like this existed at Longmire, Paradise, and at Indian Henry's Hunting Ground, a six-mile hike from Longmire.

This is the Longmire mountain viewing stand. Across the road is Longmire's Pool Hall. After Robert Longmire's tavern was shut down by the National Park Service, he opened this pool hall instead.

In 1904, the Tacoma Eastern Railroad reached Ashford, a small town six miles from today's Nisqually Entrance. During its first year of operation, it brought 500 visitors to the park. Ten years later, that figure climbed to over 100,000. Tourists heading to Longmire Springs or Paradise still needed horses to travel the last few miles, but the relative ease of travel lured many newcomers to the mountain.

Pictured here is a horse stage on the muddy road below Christine Falls. James Longmire often asked for help from area business leaders and organizations, such as the Washington Alpine Club and the Tacoma Academy of Science, to create wider, better roads to increase tourism. He was one of the first to promote the idea of a national park, but he died in 1897, before it became a reality.

Once Mount Rainier became the nation's fifth national park in 1899, many thought that the federal government would buy out the Longmire mineral claim, which was now inside national park boundaries. Instead, the government gave the Tacoma Eastern Railroad Company a lease to build a rival hotel immediately south of the Longmire property. This image shows their new inn, the National Park Inn, built in 1906 just in time for the Fourth of July. Three stories high, it accommodated 60 guests in more elegant style than rustic Longmire Springs. Elegant guests, such as those pictured at right, could expect electric lighting, fine dining, and more refined musical entertainment than what was commonly found around evening bonfires. Rates were $2.75 to $3 a day, which included board.

Martha Longmire is pictured here on the far right. The others are unidentified. Martha and her husband, Elcaine, were involved with the family's businesses at Longmire for many years. The resort was increasingly popular, and Martha helped with the cooking and caring for the guests' needs. Shown here is the hotel after several additions. Trail rides became an important tourist activity, but horses could also be problematic. Famous park photographer Asahel Curtis noted in 1911 that "large piles of manure are taken out of the stables at Longmire Springs and scattered over the ground." National Park Inn also had some trouble with sanitary conditions, reportedly disposing of kitchen waste in the Nisqually River. Longmire Springs, however, was increasingly the source of complaints for its relatively shabby conditions.

Two

ENTER THE AUTO

Early automobile enthusiasts formed clubs and looked for driving destinations. This picture shows an "auto stage" that brought guests to National Park Inn. Mount Rainier National Park was the first in the nation to welcome automobiles, with 60 cars entering in 1907. The next year, drivers needed an automobile permit, paying an exorbitant $5 (about the same as a day's wage for an automobile company worker).

Guests drove through old-growth forests of Douglas fir and hemlock to reach Longmire. The automobile permits issued in 1908 stipulated that cars needed to drive no more than six miles per hour (except on straight stretches), stop when teams of horses approached, and honk their horn at bends in the road to alert teams that might be approaching.

This image from August 1912 shows billboard advertising at Longmire Springs. The legible half of the sign on the left screams, "YOU ALSO NEED A COPY OF BARNES' ART BOOK," and the sign on the right reads, "Longmire Springs, Hot Mineral, Steam, Shower, Plunge Baths, Massages, Rubs, Our Specialty."

A lively group of Longmire waitresses is shown in 1912 riding in a truck marked "National Park Transportation Co." As time passed, many employees at the Longmire Springs Hotel were James Longmire's children and even grandchildren. James himself had 11 children, and his oldest son, Elcaine, had 12.

National Park Inn soon joined Longmire Springs Hotel in adding tent cabins, shown here in 1910, as an option for many guests who spent the night before heading up the Pony Trail to Paradise, which was six miles away. In the 1920s, some permanent ranger staff with families lived in the tent cabins, even through the winter, because of an employee housing shortage.

The building shown here is the library, the oldest government building in the park. It was originally built in 1910 as a community kitchen for construction workers and park employees. Later, it became a recreation room for the Youth Conservation Corps, but it is today back to another early function, that of housing reference books and some archival records.

The 1911 Longmire Clubhouse shown here was built in an early rustic design common at Mount Rainier. The Tacoma Eastern Railroad built it to provide a recreation space for guests at the National Park Inn. Douglas fir logs were used for framing and for the exterior walls. The cedar-shingle roof extends over the front entrance as a welcoming porch.

This is the interior of Longmire Clubhouse. It has a large stone chimney, a moose head mounted on the wall, Indiana hickory tables and chairs, and a soft light coming from lanterns affixed to large, vertical beams in the center of the room. National Park Inn guests listened to music by the fire in the evenings. Over the years, the building has served many additional purposes, such as a residence for the hotel manager, shops and offices, a center of information for hikers, and an employee dormitory. Today, it is attached by a walkway to the current National Park Inn and serves as a delightful general store and gift shop. The early rustic style is well suited for its national park setting. Later in the park's history, rustic style would become central to a ground-breaking master plan, the first in National Park Service history.

In 1916, the Longmire family leased their hotel operation to investors, the Longmire Springs Hotel Company. That company built the hotel pictured here, called the National Park Inn Annex. By 1919, a newly formed Rainier National Park Company came to terms with the Longmire family and investors, becoming owners of the buildings and a 20-year lease on the land.

The sign reads, "Longmire Springs Hotel," and points to the annex. What happened to the "real" Longmire Springs Hotel? In 1920, the RNPC demolished it, moved the annex across the road next to National Park Inn, and removed various outbuildings. Woods now obscure the location of the old Longmire Springs Hotel, but a plaque still marks the spot, just off the Trail of the Shadows.

The RNPC built "housekeeping cabins," shown here in 1916, to provide better overflow accommodations than the tent cabins. Ironically, roads to Paradise improved so much that Longmire soon became only a short rest stop for most people—not an overnight stay. The National Park Service became anxious to relieve congestion at Paradise and sought to rehabilitate Longmire as a health spa, but the idea was dropped when the water was retested and found to have little medicinal value. Pictured below is an accommodation to the automobile culture, the 1929 Longmire Gas Station, built in collaboration between National Park Service architects and the Associated Oil Company. It is one of three National Historic Landmarks in Longmire Village.

Pictured are the 1906 National Park Inn on the right, and the National Park Inn Annex in its new location across the road from where it was originally built in 1916. When Stephen Mather became the first head of the National Park Service in 1916, many parks, including Mount Rainier, were run by a ragtag jumble of fly-by-night concessionaires. Mather believed that bringing them under single management was the key to a positive tourist experience and the best bet for maintaining

a peaceful, "natural park" atmosphere. Businessmen from Seattle and Tacoma agreed, forming the RNPC. Tidying up Longmire was a top priority (after building Paradise Inn), and they were able, within two years, to consolidate the National Park Inn and other small businesses under its umbrella.

This small, unassuming structure was built in 1916 as the first building for administration. Even though Mount Rainier had been a national park since 1899, it was not until the National Park Service came into being that it began to leave its ragtag days of operation behind. A much bigger administration building was built in 1928, and though this small building was slated for demolition, park naturalist Frank Brockman instead advocated turning it into a museum and naturalist's office. Pictured below is the front desk at the entrance to the building. Brockman succeeded in turning it into a museum and spent much time and energy building exhibit cases and filling them with interesting collections of native flora and fauna. The upstairs housed the naturalist's office and a photography darkroom.

Three

LONGMIRE VILLAGE

A man shovels snow off the far end of National Park Inn's porch roof, captured here on Christmas Day 1912. The Longmire area, where the inn is located, receives only about five to ten feet of snow annually; Paradise, a six-mile hike and approximately 2,700 feet higher in elevation, gets seven to eight times that!

Between 1915 and 1923, guests began driving past Longmire to reach Paradise, perhaps only stopping at Longmire to use the restroom. The RNPC's National Park Inn was losing money. If the road to Longmire could be kept open in the winter, however, Longmire could become a year-round destination. The National Park Service agreed, and in 1923, it began keeping the road to Longmire open all year. The National Park Inn opened on weekends, renting out snowshoes, skis, and toboggans. In 1924, the RNPC even brought in a team of 13 Alaskan sled dogs and an Eskimo driver to take paying tourists on dogsled rides. Horse-drawn sleigh rides were also offered. Earlier, on Paradise Inn's opening day (July 1, 1917), its first tourists arrived from Longmire by sleigh due to an unusually heavy snowpack!

Pictured here is the popular toboggan run at Longmire. It was part of the RNPC's attempt to make Longmire a winter resort. Unfortunately, the snowfall is fickle at Longmire. Frequent rains and above-freezing temperatures during the winter create unpredictable conditions, while the snowfall is much more consistent and of better quality for winter sports up at Paradise. A proposal to build an aerial tramway from the bridge over the Nisqually River to carry tourists up the mountainside was made by RNPC's chairman T.H. Martin. It would operate only when the road was closed. The idea was sent to Stephen Mather at the National Park Service. It did not receive serious consideration until the RNPC was building a second hotel, the Paradise Lodge, which was intended to remain open year-round. Stephen Mather never reached a definite decision, and the RNPC eventually let the idea slide when it finished the lodge and was short on funds.

A fire destroyed the original National Park Inn in 1926. As this photograph shows, the annex was immediately renamed the National Park Inn. The dining room was changed to a cafeteria, as advertised on the building. Eight cabins (shown covered with snow), were added in 1926 over the site of the original inn. Shops and offices were moved from the annex to the clubhouse (the roof above the cabins).

The 1916 Administration Building is the small building on the left. It is shown here in its original location. The 1928 Administration Building is the large building on the right. After the original 1916 building was saved by naturalist Frank Brockman, it was moved across the street and still serves today as a museum.

These cars are parked in front of the National Park Inn. Visitors today park behind the inn. Note the skiers in the background. Cross-country skiing and snowshoeing have long been popular winter sports around Longmire, despite the fickle weather. Prior to 1923, before the road was kept open to Longmire through the winter, 1,200–1,400 people skied or snowshoed into the park each winter, especially on weekend outings.

A porch was added to the National Park Inn (the old annex) in 1926, creating a welcoming place to sit that is still there today. A kitchen was added at the same time. A sign hanging from the porch roof advertises ski rentals, which were part of the RNPC promotion of Longmire as a winter destination.

Here, the Longmire Museum (the original administration building) is in its new setting across the road from the 1928 Administration Building. The giant slice of a Douglas fir tree stationed in front has interesting dates marked on its rings. It began life in 1293 (before Christopher Columbus, but after Oxford University was established in England). It was 5.5 feet in diameter and nearly 700 years old when a storm blew it down in 1963.

These stylish visitors are considering the stages of a pinecone with the help of a park guide. After its creation in 1916, the National Park Service developed an interpretive program with the cooperation of the park concessionaire. The RNPC offered a mountain guide service, and the National Park Service's educational department handled nature talks and guided walks. At Longmire, lectures were given in the Sylvan Theater in the public campground.

In this photograph of the National Park Inn, the covered walkway to the clubhouse and the full porch added in 1926 can be seen. The original porch chairs were made by the Indiana Hickory Company. Made of hickory poles bent into shape and pegged together, their seats were often woven from the inner bark of hickory trees. Some are still in use in the park today.

Visitors who stayed in Longmire found many activities, like self-guided nature trails, guided walks, and lectures in the campground. In 1922, tennis courts were added. Cabins, like the ones pictured here, were built in the late 1920s and early 1930s. They housed the many employees who were needed to serve tourists when the park was at its busiest.

As automobile camps became popular, the tent cabins came down. At Longmire, a public campground (used today for park volunteers) was built in 1924 across the Nisqually River, accessible by suspension bridge. The original bridge was made of peeled logs. Above is the rustic-style Community Building, built in 1927, located just over the bridge. One of three National Historic Landmarks at Longmire, it has a large stone fireplace and rustic lighting. Interestingly, while it appears to be built of notched logs, it is actually a thick log veneer on the interior and exterior. The picture below shows its interior. Bette Filley, author of *The Big Fact Book of Mount Rainier*, described it as being "in constant use for social events, pot-lucks, church services, lectures, speakers, educational events, weddings, dances, and anything else that needed a good big dry room."

Here is the Administration Building, built in 1928. It was the centerpiece of a style created by the Landscape Division of the National Park Services called Park Rustic. At Mount Rainier, this meant log beams, glacial boulders, and a cedar shingle roof—elements of the wilderness setting. The simple but beautiful designs symbolized the ideals of the national park.

Captured in 1939, this photograph highlights one reason why some began to suggest that employee housing, shops, and administration headquarters should be moved outside the park to a lower elevation—unpredictable weather. One architect was also concerned with possible flooding at Longmire. The National Park Service incorporated this goal into the 1956 development plan (Mission 66), moving headquarters down the road to Ashford, Washington, in 1968.

Called the Longmire Commons, these residential cabins were built along a semicircular path lined with a rock border. Lawns and trees were planted to increase the neighborhood feel. Some were built in 1923, and others were added in 1926 as part of a master plan—the first such plan for any national park in the nation. The comprehensive plan covered all roads, concession services, and administrative facilities. Rapid growth in the number of guests meant a growing, year-round park staff. By the end of the 1920s, a quarter of a million people visited Mount Rainier National Park each year. Staff was added to accommodate visitors' needs for protection, education, landscape, maintenance, engineering, and electricity. Safe roads, clean restrooms, cafeterias, dining rooms, picnic areas, and for some, a comfortable place to stay were all expected by the automobile-traveling guests.

This c. 1927 photograph shows another view of Longmire Commons. Some permanent employees had families live with them there. Beginning in the winter of 1925–1926, the National Park Inn was used as a school for some 14 children. The RNPC set up a classroom at the inn during the off season with desks, blackboards, and other needed items. The National Park Service paid half the teacher's salary. The parents paid the other half.

This is a close-up of one of the cabins in Longmire Commons. The picture is labeled, "Rental Cabin," so it is possible that not all of the cabins were used for employee housing. In the mid-1920s, some employee families were reportedly still living a rather miserable existence in tent cabins, even through the winter.

The list of new construction during the 1920s included the Administration Building, Longmire Commons, the Community Building, and others. Many workers were needed for the construction boom, and they all needed someplace other than the hotel to eat. This c. 1928 image shows the construction workers' mess hall. The nearby library served as a kitchen at the time.

The 1930s brought a new group of hardworking young men to Mount Rainier. This is a CCC group in 1935. There were eight CCC camps around the mountain, with nearly 1,600 young men arriving by train from throughout the country, even from as far away as New York City.

Note the rugged landscape and tent platforms on stilts that formed the CCC Narada Falls Camp. At Longmire, they used plans provided by the National Park Service's Design and Engineering Branch based in San Francisco and built some of the cottages.

At this tent camp at Narada Falls, a First Aid sign is clearly visible on the right. Given the nature of CCC work, it was most likely in high demand! The young men maintained hundreds of miles of trails, improved campgrounds and picnic areas, completed revegetation projects, and built bridges, patrol cabins, and fire lookouts. They often had to hike to remote areas to do their job for the day.

Eugene Ricksecker, an army engineer with the task of designing and building the first real road in the park, largely followed the popular route originally blazed by James Longmire. He challenged his head surveyor to take the road past as many points of interest as possible, like Christine Falls, which visitors still experience today.

The volcanic and glacial scenery is stunningly beautiful, but geohazards can play havoc with road structures. In 1932, the Nisqually Bridge (shown here) was washed out by a 20-foot-high wall of water, catching a picnicking family on shore by surprise and marooning guests at Paradise Inn. Twice more, while workmen rushed to put in a temporary bridge, water came rushing down the mountain.

Four

PARADISE FOUND
AND DEVELOPED

Rainier National Park Company investors proudly displayed this drawing after they successfully completed the risky and bold experiment of building Paradise Inn and Annex at such high altitude. The summer season—that time when "the flowers and the glaciers meet"—is very short at Paradise, and when narrow, snow-covered roads refused to melt until July, it was a challenge to simply get guests to their hotel rooms in the early years.

Photographed around 1941, this image displays the valley that inspired one of the Longmire women to exclaim, "This is paradise!" Depending on the source, sometimes Virinda, James Longmire's wife, is given credit for naming the valley, and some say it was Elcaine Longmire's wife, Martha. (Interestingly, one source named each woman in different chapters of the book!) The Longmire family, especially Ben Longmire, named many sights around Mount Rainier.

When Eugene Ricksecker designed the road to Paradise in 1903, very few people in Washington State owned a car. Accordingly, he created a gentle grade—"the steepest up which teams can trot"—that would keep visitors "in a keen state of expectancy" as the road wound up the mountain. 1910 was the first full season that horse-drawn vehicles, like this one, could travel the road all the way to Paradise.

Pictured above is the Comstock family in 1895 in front of a tent camp hotel on Theosophy Ridge in Paradise Valley. They opened a coffee shop, which they called Paradise Hotel, and Capt. James Skinner operated a nearby tent camp on Alta Vista. Another tent camp in the park in these early days was the Wigwam Hotel, located at Indian Henry's Hunting Ground, established in 1908 by George B. Hall and Susan Longmire Hall. Both hotels were accessed by trails of approximately six miles in length from Longmire. Indian Henry's Hunting Ground is very beautiful, but early on, people decided that Paradise's subalpine meadows were the desired destination. ("Indian Henry" was the American name given to the Native American Satulick.)

In 1898, John L. Reese combined both the coffee shop and tent camp into one business for tourists called Camp of the Clouds. Each July, he packed in supplies and set up camp. At times, he encountered deep snow on the trail as late as mid-July. To prepare the tent sites, he would use horse-drawn road scrapers and dynamite to clear out the wet, condensed snow. Park officials held him in high regard.

Reese officially obtained a permit in 1902 from the US secretary of the interior. It allowed him to occupy two acres on Theosophy Ridge and provide tents, bedding, and board to tourists. He was also sometimes given permission to graze two milk cows and six horses. In 1916, the RNPC bought the camp and continued to use it to house Paradise Inn construction crews.

Early visitors, like these at Paradise River, were often drawn to Paradise by the trails, rushing streams, and wildflowers, just like today. Getting there, however, was sometimes an expedition! Naturalist Floyd Schmoe recalled a four-hour train trip in the winter of 1919 to get from Seattle to Ashford and then a 13-mile sled ride to Longmire, followed by a 6-mile hike on snowshoes up to Paradise.

Early climbers formed the Washington Alpine Club in 1891, the Mazamas in 1894, and then the Mountaineers in 1906. The Mountaineers have been a leading organization helping park officials embrace the national park goal of preserving the wilderness. Preserving the wilderness at Mount Rainier often conflicted with goals like improving road access throughout the park. The Mountaineers helped officials understand the environmental impact of their decisions, and still do so today.

Every visitor to Paradise in the summer hopes to catch wildflowers in bloom. Bear grass, shown here, only blooms every five to seven years, but as plants are on different cycles, there will usually be bear grass in bloom someplace. Naturalist Floyd Schmoe noted that local Indians came to the high meadows each year to gather the long, straight stems for their basket-making.

Hoary marmots have long delighted Paradise visitors, coming out of burrows or playing in a meadow. They whistle shrilly to warn of potential predators. The National Park Service describes them as having "grizzled grey fur on their shoulders and upper back, which fades to brown on the lower back." They eat meadow plants as fast as they can to help them survive a long hibernation.

The Nisqually Entrance Arch, shown here, is identical to the original pergola that was erected in 1911. After US Secretary of the Interior Richard A. Ballinger visited the park in 1910, he requested the construction of a rustic gateway. It was completed in time for President Taft's visit in October the next year.

Horse traffic was allowed to Paradise in 1910; the first cars—the first to enter any national park—could drive as far as Nisqually Glacier in 1908 and as far as Narada Falls in 1909. Automobiles did not regularly travel the narrow road all the way to Paradise until 1915. President Taft's 1911 visit, shown here, required his automobile to be pulled by mules part of the distance.

William Howard Taft was the US secretary of war when the road project to Paradise was initiated and was the person who had assigned the task of building it to the Army Corps of Engineers. It was fitting, then, for him to visit the road himself and have the honor of reaching Paradise in an automobile. Before heading to the subalpine meadows and Camp of the Clouds, Taft had lunch at National Park Inn. The following year, he wrote to the secretary of the interior, supporting further road development: "I promised that this should be done when I was in Washington the last time. The proximity of the great National Park, with its beautiful mountain scenery, to two large cities like Tacoma and Seattle justifies an immediate expenditure for bringing the Park within the reach of the humblest citizen."

The first road from Narada Falls to Paradise Valley was narrow and dangerous. Automobile traffic was tightly controlled. Stages left Nisqually Glacier and Paradise on the hour and passed Narada Falls on the half hour. Women and boys under 21 were warned by a sign posted at Nisqually Glacier not to drive past that point. A woman apparently almost drove her car off a cliff once, and park administrators decided that women suffered dizziness "looking over steep areas." Eugene Ricksecker had originally tried to avoid building such a narrow road, but he did not have the funds to carry out his plan all the way to Paradise. Automobile clubs in Seattle and Tacoma kept up the pressure to improve the road, but when jurisdiction was transferred from the Department of War to the Department of the Interior, it caused some delay. Shown here, the road was finally widened after World War I, when people's enthusiasm for automobiles and the outdoors combined with the government generously supporting road development. Between 1915 and 1929, the numbers of people visiting the park exploded from 30,000 to 250,000.

Camp of the Clouds, pictured above, operated under the assumption that people either arrived on foot or by horse. They came with just a few changes of clothes, and meals were prepared for them at reasonable rates. In 1914, two people could rent a tent, which included their meals, for $2.50 per day per person, or $14 per week per person. Once cars began coming up the road, however, campers came more prepared. They could cook for themselves or purchase meals separately from Reese's camp. Breakfast was 50¢, and lunch and dinner were both 75¢. As the picture below shows, auto camping became very popular—so popular that Camp of the Clouds soon became obsolete.

ECTION OF PARADISE VALLEY CAMP GROUND. TATOOSH RANGE IN BACKGROUND. Rainier National Park.

In 1915, when private, local investors formed the RNPC, their first priority was to build a first-class inn at Paradise. To locate the best site, they drove as far as possible, walked to the hilltop where they could see the mountain, the valley, and the Tatoosh Range, and someone said, "Why not here?" They opened for business on July 1, 1917. Tacoma architect Frederick Heath designed the inn. It had 37 guest rooms and a dining room for 400. Automobile stages, pictured above and below, organized by tour companies, brought well-heeled guests. A *Seattle Daily Times* article noted that visitors were brought up from Longmire by sleigh on Paradise Inn's opening day due to the heavy snowpack that year.

As seen in this photograph of the Paradise Inn lobby, the interior framework of the building is exposed and comprised of weathered Alaska yellow cedar. The huge logs support the roof when the snow piles up and are from an area below Narada Falls called the Silver Forest. The trees had been burned, weathered to a fine silver, and then felled during road construction to Paradise.

In this lobby image, note the "throne chair" at left, the huge grandfather clock in the back, the immense table at center, and the piano at right. German carpenter Hans Fraehnke (from Fife) spent seven years crafting rustic furnishings for the lobby out of the Alaska yellow cedar from the Silver Forest. For the piano, he fitted the cedar around a commercial piano.

The "tree stump" mailbox design shown here was also by Hans Fraehnke. It fits in well with the rustic lobby and other furniture designed by the German carpenter. Incidentally, mail delivery in the early days was not easy. Bette Filley's *Big Fact Book of Mount Rainier* tells of an 11-year-old boy from Ashford who was paid $1 plus dinner to deliver Paradise's mail on foot.

These writing tables at Paradise Inn were also created by Hans Fraehnke. This is a view of the first floor of the inn, looking south. The very heavy tables are still there today. Also, stairs are now at the far end that go up to a mezzanine level, which was added sometime after this photograph was taken.

The large addition to Paradise Inn shown here is the 104-room annex, built by the RNPC in 1920. After a lull during World War I, the profitable season of 1919 encouraged the company to expand. Next to the inn and barely distinguishable is the roof of the Tatoosh Club, a women's dormitory for seasonal employees. That and a men's dormitory, pictured below, called the Sluiskin Club, were built concurrently with the construction of Paradise Inn. They each had steeply pitched gable roofs lacking eaves, shiplap siding, and small, double-hung windows. The Sluiskin Club was named for the famous Indian guide who led Hazard Stevens and Philemon Beecher Van Trump on the first recorded climb to the top of Mount Rainier. Note the doors to nowhere on the second and third floors; could these be ground level during winter snow?

Prior to the annex, 125 bungalow tents occupied the slopes to the south and east of the inn. Each contained two double beds and a canvas partition down the middle. Rates for the tents were much less expensive than at the inn, but as soon as demand justified it, the RNPC built the annex and ended tent camping around Paradise Inn.

This view of Paradise Inn includes the enclosed skybridge built to connect the inn to its annex. It created a seamless corridor that adds to the charm of the old structures; indeed, visitors often cannot tell which building their room is in. The Paradise Guide House is also seen at far left. It was built at the same time as the annex.

In this publicity photograph of two bears "kissing" a man on the steps of a Paradise building, guests were seemingly encouraged to interact with wildlife. The inn offered rides for a dollar to an open garbage pit near Paradise Inn where bears were frequent visitors. A sign read, "No bear. No fare." Naturalist Floyd Schmoe called the bears "wandering mendicants," begging for food.

Publicity became increasingly important to the Rainier National Park Company. It was difficult to make a profit during the short summer season, so they turned to publicity photographs and other advertising methods to draw tourists, including East Coast visitors, to their properties. Radio concerts were one such attempt. This picture shows Seattle's KOMO radio team at Paradise for a broadcast of some kind.

The surging popularity of the tent camps and Paradise Inn, in large part due to the improved road, caused the RNPC to also expand its facilities in 1918 with Paradise Camp Lodge (not to be confused with later Paradise Lodge). Paradise Camp Lodge was located about 700 feet southwest of Paradise Inn. It was originally intended to serve as a check-in station and to serve nearby campers in canvas tent cabins, but it was expanded in the 1920s to include hotel accommodations. The picture above from the late 1920s shows the building after the expansion. Individual automobiles now made their way up to Paradise in droves. The tent cabins are clearly visible to the right and left behind the lodge. The sign on the close-up of Paradise Camp Lodge below advertises meals, tents, supplies, rooms, and souvenirs.

Always evolving, the developed area at Paradise has been under construction many times, but this was especially true from the 1920s to early 1930s. Paradise Camp Lodge, shown in the background at left, more than doubled in size. At the end of the 1920s, the RNPC looked to expand its accommodations for guests yet again, but this time to specifically develop a premier ski resort. With the approval of the National Park Service, they built Paradise Lodge on the far western side of the Paradise developed area. They hoped that it would not be subject to the same level of drifting there as at Paradise Inn, which was literally covered by drifts all winter. Paradise Lodge was completed in 1928. The photograph below shows the building in full use. Soon after it was built, the RNPC added 275 housekeeping cabins all around the new lodge. These replaced the tent cabins at Paradise Camp Lodge. Paradise Lodge had a camp store and cafeteria, which offered guests a less formal option for meals.

This photograph of a couple on the porch of Paradise Lodge shows the lodge's spectacular view of the mountain. Clearly visible also are familiar-looking trails through the wildflower meadows that had already been formed by the early 1930s.

Taken from inside Paradise Lodge cafeteria, this photograph shows two guests enjoying the view of the mountain while they eat. Two of the housekeeping cabins are visible, which were constructed to accommodate guests throughout the 1930s. The cafeteria-style dining added a less formal option for all tourists than the dining room at Paradise Inn.

In the heart of the Depression, Paradise Inn stood largely empty. The RNPC, trying to stay afloat, changed its approach to entice a larger local crowd, rather than maintaining its typical promotions to Easterners. They lowered rates and set up 275 housekeeping cabins, pictured here, near the new Paradise Lodge, and only opened Paradise Inn to overflow guests on summer weekends. This lasted just one season. Considered a step up from the canvas bungalow tents of the previous decade, the RNPC ultimately realized that the cabins needed to be upgraded or removed completely. The RNPC sold them in 1943 for $160 each. The military snatched them up to house Puget Sound defense workers. Many of the cabins also became housing for migrant workers in Yakima Valley. Below is a publicity photograph of one of the cabins.

Pictured above, the Tatoosh Range rises behind the Community Building (left) and Paradise Lodge (right). Built by 1926, the Community Building, also called "Community House," joined a comfort station, store, and ranger cabin in the area; the store and ranger station were removed after Paradise Lodge was built in 1928. The picture below shows a close-up of the Community Building. It was used for indoor recreation, including motion picture shows for the CCC boys, and popular lectures by rangers and naturalists.

At right stands the 1920 Guide House. In the distance, Paradise Camp Lodge can be seen in its original 1918 configuration, prior to a large addition. Built to maintain stylistic compatibility with the nearby lodges, it housed a guide service run by the Rainier National Park Company. It developed a very professional reputation for its summit and glacier guided climbs.

Photographer Ira Spring described in Ruth Kirk's book *Sunrise to Paradise: The Story of Mount Rainier National Park* that the photographers would take a picture of a group just heading out and then run ahead up the trail to take more pictures of them at scenic places along the way, including the Ice Caves. By the time the group returned, they would find their wet photographs hanging on the Guide House wall.

A 1956 National Park Service master plan called for a day-use facility to replace, among other things, all overnight lodging at Paradise. The goal was to have this and all the other pieces of this ambitious plan in place within 10 years—thus, Mission 66. Paradise Lodge had fallen into disrepair anyway, and was burned to the ground in 1965 to make room for the new day-use visitor center.

Nestled beautifully between the Tatoosh Range and Mount Rainier at the meadow's edge, the Henry M. Jackson Visitor Center, named for the longtime Washington senator, was built in 1966. In such close proximity to the metropolitan areas of Seattle and Tacoma, thousands of visitors a year could simply drive to the park for the day. The new visitor center was designed to accommodate the needs of these day-use tourists.

Here are two good views of the original Henry M. Jackson Visitor Center interior. Very modern in design (some likened it to a flying saucer, or the top of the Space Needle), it was supposed to be reminiscent of the mountain itself—round and white and bold. It had a cafeteria, picnic areas, hot showers for climbers, and wide-open areas for the gift shop. The photograph above shows one of the ramps that circled the interior, leading from one floor to the next. A museum on the second floor featured mountaineering artifacts from early climbers, as well as educational information on the flora and fauna of the mountain.

The picture above shows part of the 360-degree panoramic view offered by the original Henry M. Jackson Visitor Center. Guests in August 1966 are seen at right enjoying the view. At the time, the building was the most expensive in the national park system. The views were stunning, and the building seemed spacious, but it was also jarringly modern compared to the more historic buildings in the area, though set apart from them. It was also very expensive to maintain. The flat, concrete roof collected snow, which had to be melted through an embedded system of hot water pipes. In the coldest weather, 500 gallons of diesel fuel per day were needed to keep the system going, according to Eric Walkinshaw, construction manager of the new Henry M. Jackson Memorial Visitor Center.

This is Ski Dorm, also called Ski Lodge. The National Park Service built it to provide affordable lodging for budget-minded groups, such as college and high school students. It opened in 1941, in the same month that the United States entered World War II. In 1964, it was converted to apartments for employee housing. Since 1996, another Ski Dorm has stood in much the same spot with an interesting drive-through feature.

This is the 1920 Guide House. A comfort station (restroom) was added by the National Park Service in 1928 to accommodate the needs of the ever-rising number of day-use visitors to the park. The tunnel allows people to use the comfort station during the winter. It extends into the plowed parking lot and allows the snow to pile around it.

Five

Summer in Paradise

With an annual average snowfall of approximately 670 inches and the possibility of snow nearly any day of the year, the seasons at Paradise are blurred, indeed. This summertime photograph shows guests arriving at Paradise Inn, which originally opened each year in July. The first cars would arrive once the road was finally cleared of snow.

Titled "Girls with Snowballs," this photograph shows two children standing in front of the snow tunnel entrance to Paradise Inn. Floyd Schmoe stayed at the inn during the winter of 1919. He kept the tunnel open as winter keeper with his young wife, Ruth. Pictured below are, from left to right, unidentified, Ruth Schmoe, daughter Esther Schmoe, Floyd Schmoe holding an ice ax, and unidentified. In *A Year in Paradise*, Floyd Schmoe wrote that they had to reopen and extend the tunnel each time it snowed. During storms, venturing even 50 feet from the tunnel's mouth could be deadly. The high winds could blow people away, Schmoe noted, exhausting them or covering them with snow before they could "fight their way back."

Guests at Paradise Inn had professional climbing guides available to them for hire. Hans Fuhrer, shown at far right, and his brother Heinie were known to be extremely good at guiding guests safely to the summit and back. Hans also had the reputation for being a witty and cheerful yodeler. The inn supplied climbers with lunches of raisins, nuts, boiled eggs, hardtack, and chocolate. Guides also got extra eggs and an orange.

Pictured around 1920 is a mixed hiking party comprised of both men and women, which was common at that time (compared to Fay Fuller's time in the late 1880s to 1890s, when it was not). The guide, third from the right, is identified by his ice ax rather than a hiking staff, which was supplied by the Guide House to every hiker in such parties.

Guests in the early days at Paradise Inn were encouraged to take guided hikes onto nearby Paradise Glacier, and that was a job for the first female guide at Mount Rainier National Park, Alma Wagen. She was a Tacoma teacher who worked as a guide in 1918. Floyd Schmoe recalled the lesson on how to slide down Pinnacle Glacier, as taught to him by a different guide: "Just sit loose. Let nature take its course. But don't roll, you might get hurt. If you start rolling, flatten out on the snow, spread-eagle, and the snow will stop you." The guide would slide first, and one at a time, the rest of the group would follow, "screaming and yelling, every which way, all over the place, but no one was hurt."

Guided walks through the wildflower-splashed meadows were also very popular. The guide at far left is identified by the rope strapped around his torso and his ice ax. Groups consisted of both men and women, all enjoying the hikes through the wildflowers together.

This photograph is labeled "Calypso" for the flower pictured. It is most often a vibrant pink, but there is a white variety as well. There are hundreds of different varieties of wildflowers in Mount Rainier National Park. John Muir, who had been on mountains all over the world, described the subalpine park at Paradise as the greatest he would ever see.

Ice caves and tunnels formed at the terminus of glaciers, like the Kautz Ice Cavern pictured here. In the summer months, melting streams emerging from the end of a glacier would meet currents of warm air, and a cave would form. Hiking to the caves was a very popular tourist activity and was one of the reasons why people drove past Longmire and up the long, winding road to Paradise.

The people in this photograph at a Paradise ice cave are on a guided tour. This was a profitable activity for the often-struggling RNPC. Cave entrances were usually buried by winter blizzards and did not open naturally until late in the summer. The RNPC sometimes tried to help nature along by chopping at the snow, or even blasting it, to make the openings large enough for people to enter in July.

Here, the guide is pointing with his ice ax at a cave feature. The incredible blue colors of the ice created long-lasting memories for tourists lucky enough to have seen them. Caves were also dangerous. Ice flakes hanging from the ceiling could fall. At least one person—who was not on a tour—was touching one when it broke off and killed him.

This undated photograph shows a man surveying one of the caves. Over eight miles were recorded and mapped; the main tunnel was over a mile long. Every year, however, the shifting glacier meant that the tunnels were a little different. As the glaciers thinned and retreated, the caves in the 1970s and 1980s became too dangerous for the public. The ceiling of the last cave collapsed in 1991.

In the 1930s, there were guides, hired by the Rainier National Park Company, and naturalists and rangers hired by the National Park Service (NPS). Pictured above is an employee of the NPS. The two groups generally cooperated, with the RNPC guides leading summit and glacier climbs and the NPS naturalists and rangers giving well-attended public lectures in the Paradise Community House and leading walks around Paradise, as pictured below. In 1933, however, the RNPC guides began giving rival lectures in the Paradise Inn lobby. Curious what would happen, the NPS pulled the plug on their talks. Public outcry demanded those lectures return, so they did. After that, the RNPC guide program and the interpretive programs by the NPS were kept better delineated. Also, NPS naturalists and rangers agreed to allow the RNPC guides several minutes to advertise their climbing services to guests at the end of NPS nature talks.

The Skyline Trail was a popular five-mile loop that took guests high above Paradise in a half-day guided trip; pictured above is its trailhead. The RNPC also featured rides to Reflection Lakes and to the foot of the Tatoosh Range. The RNPC publicity photograph at right shows a pony guide riding on top of the snow tunnel entrance to Paradise Inn—clearly an attempt to draw attention to their trail rides! Differences in purpose between park concessions (to provide access to the wilderness areas and make a profit) and National Park Service (to preserve the wilderness and encourage safe, but somewhat restricted, access) became increasingly apparent as time went on. Horses damaged the fragile meadows. In the 1970s, horse parties were limited to six horses per group and were ultimately eliminated as a park activity.

The RNPC believed a golf course at Paradise would draw tourists from the East Coast. Calling golf a "country game," Horace Albright, the director of the NPS, agreed. The RNPC opened a nine-hole course on August 1, 1931. The play was downhill, so a bus brought golfers back to the first tee. The second year, snow covered the course until mid-August, and that ended Paradise golf. Damage to the meadow from the golf course lasted decades.

Surrounded by glacial erratics, this man is fishing, something encouraged by the RNPC. Fishing began in 1915, when 25,000 nonnative eastern brook trout were poured into Mowich Lake in a different part of the park. Pack trains carried fingerling trout in bulk milk cans to be released in lakes and streams. Many decades passed before this was seen as inconsistent with the desire to preserve the wilderness and protect the animals found there.

Eugene Ricksecker, the army engineer who designed the road to Paradise, planned that the drive itself would be part of the joy of being there. Lookouts, pictured above, and other places to stop along the way, pictured below, were part of the plan. Ricksecker could probably never have foreseen how automobiles would change the pattern of tourism. Automobile stages in the photograph above show a time when people came in tour-sponsored, slow-paced groups. Tourists usually stayed overnight in a tent camp or in one of the inns or lodges. The picture below, however, shows the changing culture, which was composed of families and individuals from the nearby cities driving to Mount Rainier, picnicking, and exploring the park in their own way—often returning home the same day.

A few celebrities made it to Paradise over the years, such as Sonja Henie, John D. Rockefeller Jr., and Presidents Taft and Truman. This photograph was taken at Paradise on June 22, 1945, during Truman's postwar visit. He reportedly arrived behind the wheel of a purple convertible, along with an entourage of 55 others, including Gov. Mon C. Wallgren, reporters, a photographer, Secret Service agents, and state patrolmen. Truman threw snowballs and played in the snow, had lunch at Paradise Inn, and even played the lobby's rustic piano. The Paradise employees worked around the clock to ensure that this short visit went well. Truman met with the park superintendent and asked many questions about the National Park Service and Mount Rainier in particular. It was Truman who eventually signed a bill that allowed the National Park Service to buy out the struggling Rainier National Park Company's holdings.

Even in summer, guests could always climb a bit higher and find some snow. These images show the RNPC scheme in 1923–1924 to increase tourism by bringing a real Alaskan dog-sled team, complete with their sled and harness and Eskimo driver Dan Cakkasonoroc, to Paradise. The team posed for publicity photographs, such as the images shown here. Note the dog-sled team perched on the snow-covered roof of Paradise Inn, and an igloo constructed behind the girls with parasols below. The malamutes and Siberian huskies were brought down from Point Barrow, Alaska, and shown all around Puget Sound to promote the rides. The dogs ate so much, however, that there was no money to be made from this endeavor, and the program soon ended.

The girls in the publicity photograph above are showing off their "tin pants," which were worn for "nature coasting" (below). Tin pants were breeches with paraffin ironed into the seat, a chore performed by guides in the Guide House. Floyd Schmoe described nature coasting: "On long gentle slopes we all sat down with each man holding the feet of the one behind him. When all were ready the guide in front would lift his feet and the guide behind would shove off and the entire party would serpentine down the glacier whooping and yelling. It was good sport and no one was ever hurt much." The snowpack around Paradise Glacier was the scene of much nature coasting. Free of "large crevasses and no floating rock," the ice and snow were safe for sliding.

Nature Coasting in Summer, Paradise Glacier — Rainier National Park.

Six

WINTER IN PARADISE

This fascinating photograph was probably taken sometime around 1931, since the layout of the buildings closely matches a map of Paradise prepared for an archaeology report in 1931. Paradise Inn, the Guide House, and comfort station are clearly visible on the left in the distance. To the right of that is Paradise Camp Lodge. At right center is Paradise Lodge and Community House. Housekeeping cabins and other small buildings are hidden under the snow.

This rustic-style ranger station was built in 1921. It is one of three early Paradise buildings actually built by the National Park Service. Two others are the tow building and comfort station. Heavy snowpack hid many buildings when Floyd Schmoe and his wife arrived as winter keepers of Paradise Inn. When spring came, they enjoyed watching buildings appear out of snowdrifts—buildings they did not even know were there! The ranger station housed an emergency phone line and served as a first aid room. Injuries during the winter when people came to Paradise for skiing and sliding were common. For a time, the National Park Service wondered if monitoring a sliding area was suitable for park rangers. One year it experimented with leaving the snow play area unsupervised, and injuries skyrocketed by 900 percent.

On October 13, 1954, Paradise Lodge was being prepared for winter. A temporary steel tunnel was placed in front of the main entrance to permit people to pass through the snow that would pile up around the building throughout the winter months. After installation, it was framed with wood to be more attractive.

This picture of the old Henry M. Jackson Visitor Center was taken around 1971. More than 1,000 inches of snow fell in 1970–1971, and then, a breathtaking 1,122 inches fell the following year between July 1, 1971, and June 30, 1972. That is almost 100 feet of snow!

The high walls of plowed snow in this 1921 photograph show that keeping the road open to Paradise was not easy. Huge annual snowfall, however, seemed to beg for Paradise to become a winter sports destination. Guests could ski for months, if only they could get there. Could the National Park Service afford to keep the road open all winter? Alternatively, the RNPC had a plan to build a tram that would simply carry skiers above the snow from Nisqually Glacier to the new Paradise Lodge. By the time the lodge was built in 1928, however, the RNPC was out of funds for building the tram. The stock market crash the following year settled the matter for good.

Paradise did become the premier ski destination for the Pacific Northwest for a time, tram or no tram. The RNPC convinced the National Park Service to keep the road open all winter, which was achieved, but inconsistently. Judging from the crowds pictured in these photographs, skiers had no problem getting to the slopes at least on this day. Note also the small building in front of Paradise Inn in the photograph above. It housed the eight-cylinder Ford engine that powered the towrope and was built by the Civilian Conservation Corps. The towrope could carry 250 skiers per hour up to the saddle of Alta Vista from the Guide House.

Some predicted that Mount Rainier would become the most prominent ski resort in the nation, and ski clubs pressured the park officials and the RNPC to build modern ski lifts. The towrope was installed for the 1937–1938 ski season. Other lifts, such as T-bars, chair lifts, and trams, were nearly added, or were at least approved, over time but were never actually built. Skiers could take the lift from the Guide House to Alta Vista, and from there, some would ski all the way to Narada Falls. A shuttle bus brought them back to the Guide House where they could do it all over again. Paradise Inn was kept open that year, and floodlights even made it possible for night skiing. (Both, courtesy of the Hellyer family.)

This 1950s photograph of Ruth Kirk, author of *Sunrise to Paradise: The Story of Mount Rainier National Park*, was taken by her daughter Louise. Paradise Inn is almost completely buried under the snow behind her, with only the dormer windows and a chimney poking through the snow. Imagine spending a winter-long honeymoon living beneath that snowpack, like Floyd and Ruth Schmoe did in 1919 as winter keepers of Paradise Inn!

When the popularity of downhill skiing was surging in the 1930s and again after World War II in the 1940s, national parks hired ski instructors for new ski schools. Some of these instructors had fled Nazi Germany for safety in America. Austrian Otto Lang taught at Mount Rainier. Here is a 1937 ski school in session. (Courtesy of Allan Reinhart, US Department of the Interior.)

The *Seattle Post-Intelligencer* hosted the first race at Paradise in 1934. At 4.5 miles long and almost 5,000 feet in elevation drop, the Silver Skis was the longest downhill race in the country. Skiers climbed to Camp Muir for the start. The first national downhill and slalom championship followed in 1935 and served as the 1936 Olympic ski trials. The excitement was enormous, and the weekend of the event was the busiest in park history to that time. Pictured is prominent Austrian skier Hannes Schroll, second from left above and below, who taught alpine ski techniques in Yosemite. Another claim to fame—Schroll created Goofy's famous yodel for Walt Disney.

World War II brought some new demands on the national park system, from providing space for grazing animals to providing recreational opportunities for soldiers, but Mount Rainier National Park played a unique and special role on the home front. These c. 1940 pictures show some of the 1,000 men who trained at Mount Rainier and later became part of the 10th Mountain Infantry Division, which was composed of expert skiers who were eventually sent to fight in the mountains of Europe. Many were volunteers from New England ski clubs and Ivy League ski teams. Mount Rainier, known as "an arctic island in a temperate sea," offered a variety of climate zones and landscapes that proved useful for training the men and testing equipment.

The US Army rented Paradise Lodge and the Tatoosh Club, which was the new name for Paradise Camp Lodge in the early 1940s. Troops trained by camping in the snow, testing sleeping bags and snowsuits at the summit, and using their weapons in similar conditions to the mountains of Europe. They did sentry duty wearing specially designed "sleeping bags" that had legs and feet. One set of troops even circled the entire mountain (90 miles) carrying rifles and 85-pound packs. On weekends, when the public was welcome to come to the mountain for winter sports, troops helped set ski courses, provided first aid to skiers, and participated in races and jumps.

If the soldiers needed to test their weapons and clothing and other items in harsher conditions, all they needed to do was climb to a higher elevation on the mountain. It is difficult to ponder what kind of harsh conditions they found themselves tested by once they joined the battle in Europe, and many troops in the 10th Mountain Division did not make it home again. A plaque affixed to a large boulder at Paradise honors their time on the mountain and the actions they took that helped lead to the end of World War II in Italy. Find it by following Waterfall Trail to its west end.

Before 1917, there was little need to keep the road to Paradise open in the winter; people hiking up the trail on snowshoes from Longmire to Paradise did not need a road. Paradise Inn changed all of that, and the RNPC profits were tied to getting tourists to Paradise, snow or no snow. The NPS tried everything to move the white stuff, including tractors, army surplus TNT, steam shovels, and even by hand.

In 1931, the National Park Service purchased a "SnoGo" rotary plow, pictured here, to help keep roads open year-round. The pressure mounted as RNPC facilities at Paradise expanded in the 1920s, and again when Mount Rainier hosted nationally important races, such as the 1934 Silver Skis event and the 1936 Olympic ski trials. Clearing up to 35 feet of snow and debris made this a very difficult task.

Seven

SUNRISE (YAKIMA PARK)

Yakima Park, in the northeastern part of Mount Rainier, was one of three sites chosen in the late 1920s for possible hotel development. The RNPC hoped to reduce the pressure on the land and resources of popular Paradise. People from eastern Washington also wanted easier access to the mountain. The other two sites, Spray Park and Sunset Park, were never developed. This postcard image shows Yakima Park's obvious appeal.

Thomas Vint, director of the National Park Service Landscape Division, oversaw what became the first long-range plan for any national park. Paradise and Longmire had originally been built up and operated by multiple concessionaires, and everyone involved wanted to avoid more haphazard development. This image shows Superintendent Owen A. Tomlinson (far left) and others at Yakima Park looking at the plan.

Once a site was chosen and the master plan was created by the National Park Service, good roads needed to be built before construction of lodge facilities could begin. In 1929, the Public Roads Bureau surveyed a route from White River to Yakima Park, and a power plant, water supply, and sewage system were installed. The Sunrise Ridge Loop is pictured here in the 1930s.

A congressional committee was eager to see for itself the unfolding of the first of its kind, unified master plan of the National Park Service. In these two images, the congressional dignitaries are arriving at Yakima Park in July 1930. A dispute regarding what to call the newly developed area resulted in keeping the native name, Yakima Park, for the land, and a new name, Sunrise, for the built-up section. Sunrise Lodge and the South Blockhouse were still unfinished, but the brand-new road took them to the highest point in Washington State accessible by paved road, an elevation of 6,400 feet. They were rewarded for their efforts with spectacular views of Mount Rainier and Emmons Glacier, the largest glacier in the lower 48 states.

The Rainier National Park Company was hopeful that railroad companies would help fund a grand hotel at Sunrise similar to those at Glacier and Yellowstone. In anticipation of this likely event, the RNPC built a day-use wing of Sunrise Lodge and opened it in mid-July 1931. Foundations were laid for the second wing of what was intended to be a U-shaped building. The railroad money fell through, and the rest of the planned 300-room hotel was never built. The lodge contained a cafeteria-style dining room, store, kitchen, post office, storage, and employee dormitory, and it still serves some of these same uses today. The image above shows some of the rental cabins. Also, automobiles are stopped at the rustic-style gas station just to the right of Sunrise Lodge. At left, a man orders food at an open window.

This is the South Blockhouse, built in 1931. For design inspiration, Thomas Vint's assistant in the National Park Service Landscape Division, Ernest A. Davidson, spent time studying photographs of pioneer architecture at the Washington State Historical Society in Tacoma. He decided on a frontier-themed blockhouse for the design. Yakima Park itself had been a peaceful area where native tribes gathered for horse racing, mock battles, and berry-picking, but struggles on the frontier between settlers and natives had been a reality in the early pioneering days around Mount Rainier. James Longmire himself, well-known to be friendly with tribal people in the area, went racing once to the safety of a similarly styled blockhouse. He did not want to go but finally went at the urging of a native friend who feared for his life.

This spectacular photograph of Yakima Park and Sunrise Village at night shows the appeal of the entire area. The National Park Service master plan failed to be fully realized due to lack of funding, but it had successfully built a community of buildings that minimized intrusion into the environment and maximized the sweeping views. Today, the scene is even more natural, as the cabins have been removed and there is no overnight lodging for guests at Sunrise. In all, relatively few tourists have spent the night at Sunrise, experiencing this sight. Financial difficulties during the 1930s caused the Rainier National Park Company to sell off the 215 cabins to house migrant workers in eastern Washington and defense workers in Puget Sound. By the end of World War II, they were gone.

Behind Sunrise Lodge in this 1935 photograph, the rental cabins are visible. The Rainier National Park Company set up 215 cabins in tight rows to accommodate overnight guests. A cabin could be rented for $2.50 per day with blankets and linen, or $1.50 per day without. Guests could also rent bathtub, shower, and laundry facilities. Yakima Park was often sunnier and drier than Paradise, and the first year it was open for visitors, it was very popular. Paradise, however, with its ice caves, the preferred climbing route to the summit, subalpine meadows, and the charming inn, continued over time to be the most popular location for tourists at Mount Rainier National Park. The gas station can be seen at far right below.

Here is a close-up view of some of the cabins available for tourists to rent at Sunrise. Since the lodge was never fully developed, there was no overnight lodging in Sunrise Lodge except for employees. Although the cabins were removed in the 1940s, there is still evidence of the grid today. The light, volcanic soil is easily damaged and can take decades to repair.

The Sunrise gasoline station incorporates rustic design elements, like log framing, a gabled shake roof, and stone walls. Rustic design became an important national park concept; tourists began to expect that buildings would be made of local materials and harmonize with the environment. Gasoline sales here ended in 1979.

The Camper's Shelter is shown here under construction between the completed North and South Blockhouses. Each building stands alone. Funding for the buildings had fallen through during the Great Depression, but they were finally completed in 1943. The Camper's Shelter is known today as the Sunrise Visitor Center, and an interior image is seen below. The rustic log construction is easily seen in the interior image. An architecture guide on the park says it is made of lodgepole pine. Today, the visitor center looks much the same and houses interpretive exhibits and book sales. Guided nature walks are available daily from the visitor center during the summer season. Looking out the window, where the man using the binocular-type telescope is standing, the immense Emmons Glacier and the mountain can be seen.

Longmire and Paradise are now open year-round, but Sunrise is still the last to open and first to close each year. The historical image above shows workers preparing to clear snow from the parking lot at Sunrise for its opening day. The picture below shows a cross-country skier hitting a trail at Sunrise. In the past, snowshoers and skiers were the only ones able to travel within the park during the winter, but today, hikers are also able to venture there. However, despite the good roads and communication systems available in the park, weather conditions can quickly turn dangerous.

Horseback riding was very popular all around Mount Rainier National Park for many years and had been a special part of tribal life in the Sunrise area long before that. The Yakima tribe called the meadows of Yakima Park Me-yah-ah-Pah, which means "place of the chief," and brought herds of horses there for an annual horse-racing event. At Me-yah-ah-Pah, the horses found ample grazing land. Pictured above is the Sunrise Horse Barn in 1947. A half-day horse trip was $3. Sunrise stopped operating a horse concession in the 1960s, but the trail damage is still plainly visible from the lodge. The photograph below shows a guided horse tour above Yakima Park and Sunrise Lodge and the view from the ridge. Today, Sunrise, like Paradise, is valued for its summer wildflowers and fragile subalpine ecosystem. Designated hiking trails help to protect the area.

Eight

OHANAPECOSH

Taidnapam tribal member Jim Yoke and his family, pictured here, lived near Ohanapecosh. The name is a Taidnapam tribal word interpreted variously as "Oh, look!" or "Standing on the lip of a rock" (on which to dipnet fish). Ohanapecosh might be from an Upper Cowlitz tribal word for "clear stream" or "deep blue." The beautiful, blue-green Ohanapecosh River rushed past a hot springs resort that developed in the northeast corner of the park.

In 1906, Packwood resident John Snyder found the hot springs, and despite government opposition, he and a partner built a trail, cabin, and bath hole. Then, in 1912, Eva O'Neill set up a tent camp for hardy tourists who hiked or rode in on horseback. As tourism around Mount Rainier increased, concern for people's safety in the wilderness also increased. In 1912, park superintendent Edward Hall paid hunters to trap and kill predators. Ben Longmire, grandson of James Longmire, is shown here with a dead cougar over his shoulder. Five cougars were caught in the Ohanapecosh area in just three days in 1925. At the time, this was outside park boundaries. Ohanapecosh did not become part of Mount Rainier National Park until boundaries were enlarged in 1931. Today, of course, no animal, large or small, can be killed at Mount Rainier National Park without severe consequences, such as large fines and even jail time.

A man from Morton named N.D. Tower built a hotel and bath facility at the Ohanapecosh mineral springs in 1921. Three years later, he and Dr. Albert W. Bridge, an Eatonville and Tacoma doctor, became business partners. Over time, they built a larger hotel and two bathhouses and renamed it the Bridge Clinic. When a good road opened between Packwood and Ohanapecosh in 1933, tourism increased, and they enlarged their facilities again. The image above shows the lodge with some of the 30 cabins in the background and a bathhouse. Below is a close-up of the lodge's rustic-style construction. It was positioned against a sloping bank of the Ohanapecosh River, giving guests a beautiful view of the mountain stream. Blue-green pools and rushing white water splashing around glacial boulders are part of the scenery.

"Taking the waters" at Ohanapecosh became popular with people seeking to soak away their rheumatism and other problems in the 85-to-120-degree water. Pictured above is one of the bathhouses. The water was said to have healing properties and contained sodium, silica, iron, calcium, potassium, and other minerals. Pictured below are a few of the 30 guest cabins that were added to the development as the facility expanded in 1933. During the Depression, many people reportedly stayed for weeks and months, seeking relief for whatever ailed them by soaking in the warm water bubbling up from the ground.

From 1933 to 1941, Mount Rainier hosted eight Civilian Conservation Corps camps of up to 200 men in each. Ohanapecosh hosted a summer work camp. Hardworking young men built the original campground, a ranger and checking station, a log cabin, the Silver Falls Loop trail, and more. Pictured here is the "Forest House" museum, constructed from two CCC buildings. In 1937, park superintendent William S. Nowlin described the work at Ohanapecosh CCC camp: "One day we will be planting delicate, lacy ferns . . . the next we will be digging with a steam shovel. . . . We build huge log tables, so heavy the people can't move them around." The CCC boys pictured below have baseball bats in hand. They worked hard and played hard, too!

By 1947, Dr. Bridge suffered a stroke and sold his interest in the springs. The property fell into decline and was considered something of an embarrassment to the park compared to the rest of the developed areas and was closed in 1960. By 1967, the hotel, bathhouses, and cabins were removed, and the National Park Service allowed the springs to return to their natural state. This was also the fate of a much smaller hot springs operation not far away and up a hill. Pictured here is the modern Ohanapecosh Visitor Center, which sits adjacent to a popular campground along the Ohanapecosh River. Today, the only evidence left of the hot springs resort is a large, grassy area with warm water still streaming throughout. A travertine, or a natural build-up of minerals, fills a nearby slope.

Nine

TRAMS, CHAIRLIFTS, AND HIGH-RISE ASPIRATIONS

This 1908 postcard image of a grand, four-winged luxury spa with extensive landscaped grounds at Longmire depicts a plan that may have surpassed even the Longmire family's fondest hopes, but whose plan was it? The Rainier National Park Company, overseer of much park development, did not yet exist. The source has been lost to history, but it was, perhaps, a railroad company proposal.

Many park aspirations centered on easier access to the wonders of the mountain. The Longmires' trail to Paradise and the earliest road, like the one pictured above, were usually muddy, dusty, or covered by several feet of snow. After James's death, when a modern road was finally completed, Virinda Longmire rode in a "two-seated covered surry" between Longmire and Narada Falls. Tears streamed down her face nearly all the way. She kept saying, "To think this has come to pass—a reality. A road to Narada and Paradise. Oh Jim, Jim, if you could be with me here today in all this luxury of which we so long ago dreamed." The image below proves their dream that summer sunshine, combined with good roads, would mean full parking lots at Paradise for decades!

Chair lifts for skiers have been proposed periodically, as have different types of trams, also known as trolleys or streetcars. In 1921, the Mount Rainier National Park Advisory Board recommended a cogwheel tram from Paradise to the summit for non-climbers. A civil engineer from Seattle in a 1947 *Seattle Times* article envisioned a tram with three aluminum coaches. It was to travel above and underground 300 times a year, six times a day. A funicular (cable railway) was proposed in 1940 to carry skiers above Paradise, and in 1960, a tram was proposed to take climbers to Camp Muir, a common way-station on the standard route to the summit situated at 10,000 feet, pictured at right.

CAMP MUIR CABIN, Elevation 10,000 feet, Rainier National Park

Maj. Hiram Chittenden, namesake of the Ballard Locks in Seattle, supervised road work at Mount Rainier from 1906 to 1908. He proposed a 100-mile road that would allow cars (such as the one above at Paradise) to travel from the "snout of each glacier," from one viewpoint to another. Concerned conservationists objected. Instead of a road suitable for cars, the proposed route became the 93-mile Wonderland foot trail. At one time, people traveled it on horseback. Eugene Ricksecker, road-builder to Paradise, also mapped out an interesting road—one that led all the way to the summit. It followed the Gibralter Rock climbing route. Snowsheds were to protect the road from avalanches.

Many concessionaire aspirations for profits were dashed as winter storms delayed tourist activities and wreaked havoc on roofs, requiring expensive repairs. The image above shows Paradise Inn lying in a vice-grip of deep snow, and the image below of Paradise Lodge shows winter damage to the buildings at Paradise. Entire dormer windows at Paradise Inn were sometimes shorn off. Floyd Schmoe and his wife, Ruth, when employed as winter caretakers at the inn, were often amazed (and relieved) that the groaning roof did not collapse entirely. By the mid-1900s, park officials were making plans to give up on hotels at Paradise altogether, creating day-use only services. Paradise Lodge was the first to fall. Not as charming or as well-built as Paradise Inn, Paradise Lodge was burned down in the mid-1950s to make room for the day-use Henry M. Jackson Visitor Center.

Still, wintry weather and heavy use by tourists caught up to the aging Paradise Inn by the mid-1950s. Something had to be done. One plan was to eliminate all overnight lodging at Paradise once and for all, as at Sunrise. The other proposal is shown in this 1957 drawing. Paradise Inn would be replaced by a modern, high-rise hotel. Ten stories high with two large wings out to either side, the first four levels would sit below snow level during the winter, and all the guest rooms would be above the typical snow line. The plan was scrapped, however, when the public heard of it. The resulting outcry made it clear that the old inn was a beloved treasure. Instead of being bulldozed, the beautiful, rustic-style Paradise Inn was restored. Restoration projects to strengthen the building are ongoing, and the inn is protected as part of a National Historic District.

For years, the RNPC was interested in ways to lure vacationing Easterners to Mount Rainier, and golf was one of their favorite tourist activities. Before Paradise's failed experiment (shown in this c. 1931 image), the RNPC proposed a miniature golf course be implemented at Yakima Park. The landscape architect was enthralled with bringing golf to the sweeping meadows there. If only it was irrigated, he thought, the area "would make one of the most wonderful golf courses in the world." Another, very ambitious plan was to build several new hotels at Yakima, Sunset, and Spray Parks. Railroad companies backed grand hotels like those at Glacier and Yellowstone National Parks. Why not at Mount Rainier? Hopeful, the RNPC met in 1929 with Northern Pacific, Great Northern, Union Pacific, and Milwaukee Railroad representatives. Collaboration looked promising, and the railroad company presidents met again to discuss the idea further. The stock market crashed, however, and the grand hotels were never built. Sunrise Lodge, part of this plan, was never finished except for one wing to serve day-use tourists.

Early copper prospectors dreamed of striking it rich along the White River at Glacier Basin. Eventually, all the old claims merged with the Storbo Mine. The new company put up a blacksmith shop, saw mill, and even the hotel and boardinghouse seen above. The date of its demise, shown below, is unclear. According to some sources, the building was never used as a hotel before succumbing to bad weather. Developers marketed nearby Sunrise as a dude ranch with "real cowboys" and offered a moonlit horse trip to the "Ghost Gold Mine," at Storbo. These romantic, frontier-themed images fit in well with Sunrise's blockhouse style. The Storbo Mine is sometimes erroneously mentioned in reference material as "Starbo," and one urban legend relates the naming of the Seattle-based Starbucks coffee company to this old mining camp.

This drawing depicts a proposed development at the Mowich entrance on the western side of the park. The RNPC had big plans for Yakima Park in the east, and Spray and Sunset Parks to the west. Their hoped-for railroad partnership failed as the Great Depression hit, however, and today, the road to Mowich Lake is still unpaved just a few miles past the entrance.

The Ohanapecosh developed area (shown here in 1960, shortly before being torn down) was always simpler in scale than other developed areas in the park. Even so, it nearly became the only tourist site in the park with a swimming pool. The pool was planned and begun in the early 1930s, but, like many Depression era plans, the idea was scrapped and the pool was never finished.

People who have climbed to the summit of Mount Rainier and people who have dreamed of roads or trams to take them to the top; people who have been to the mountain hundreds of times, and people who have just gazed at it through an office window—all who have experienced the glory of seeing the snow-capped peak against a bright blue sky can say the same thing: when the mountain is out, it is a great day. Even when it is shrouded by gray clouds, we know that it is there. And we love it. We share this affection with all those who took days to get there, and with all those who will visit the park after us. May we have the vision to preserve Mount Rainier National Park for them, as others did for us. Stay for an hour or stay for days, the mountain awaits.

BIBLIOGRAPHY

Allaback, Sarah, Victoria Jacobson, and Ronald Warfield. *100 Years at Longmire Village*. Seattle, WA: Northwest Interpretive Association.

Burtchard, Greg, Benjamin Diaz, and Kendra Carlisle. "Paradise Camp: Archaeology in the Paradise Developed Area, Mount Rainier National Park." National Park Service, 2008.

Catton, Theodore R. *National Park, City Playground: Mount Rainier in the Twentieth Century*. Seattle, WA: University of Washington Press, 2006.

Filley, Bette. *The Big Fact Book About Mount Rainier: Fascinating Facts, Records, Lists, Topics, Characters, and Stories*. Issaquah, WA: Dunamis House, 1996.

Hooper, Dean, and Roberta B. Longmire. *Yelm Pioneers and Followers: 1850–1950*. Yelm, WA: Prairie Historical Society, 1999.

Kaiser, Harvey H. *An Architectural Guidebook to the National Parks: California, Oregon, Washington*. Salt Lake City, UT: Gibbs Smith, 2002.

Kirk, Ruth. *Sunrise to Paradise: The Story of Mount Rainier National Park*. Seattle, WA: University of Washington Press, 1999.

Martinson, Arthur D. *Wilderness Above the Sound: The Story of Mount Rainier National Park*. Flagstaff, AZ: Northland Press, 1986.

Rice, Marie Bauer. *James Longmire and His Dreams*. James Longmire Family of Washington State Association, 2009.

Schmoe, Floyd. *A Year in Paradise*. Seattle, WA: Mountaineers Books, 1979.

Discover Thousands of Local History Books
Featuring Millions of Vintage Images

Arcadia Publishing, the leading local history publisher in the United States, is committed to making history accessible and meaningful through publishing books that celebrate and preserve the heritage of America's people and places.

Find more books like this at
www.arcadiapublishing.com

Search for your hometown history, your old stomping grounds, and even your favorite sports team.

Consistent with our mission to preserve history on a local level, this book was printed in South Carolina on American-made paper and manufactured entirely in the United States. Products carrying the accredited Forest Stewardship Council (FSC) label are printed on 100 percent FSC-certified paper.

MADE IN THE